Under The Sea Colouring Book

Ocean Colouring Books Animals for Children Ages 2-4

Copyright © 2019 by Daniel Mandalas. All rights reserved.

No part of this book may be reproduced in any form or by any electronic or mechanical means, including information storage and retrieval systems, without written permission from the author, except for the use of brief quotations in a book review

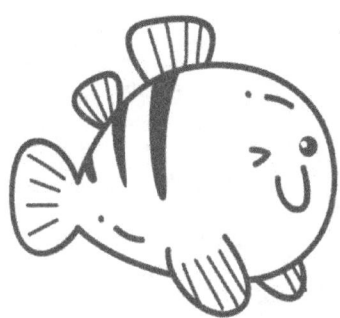

This Coloring Book Belongs To :

....

....

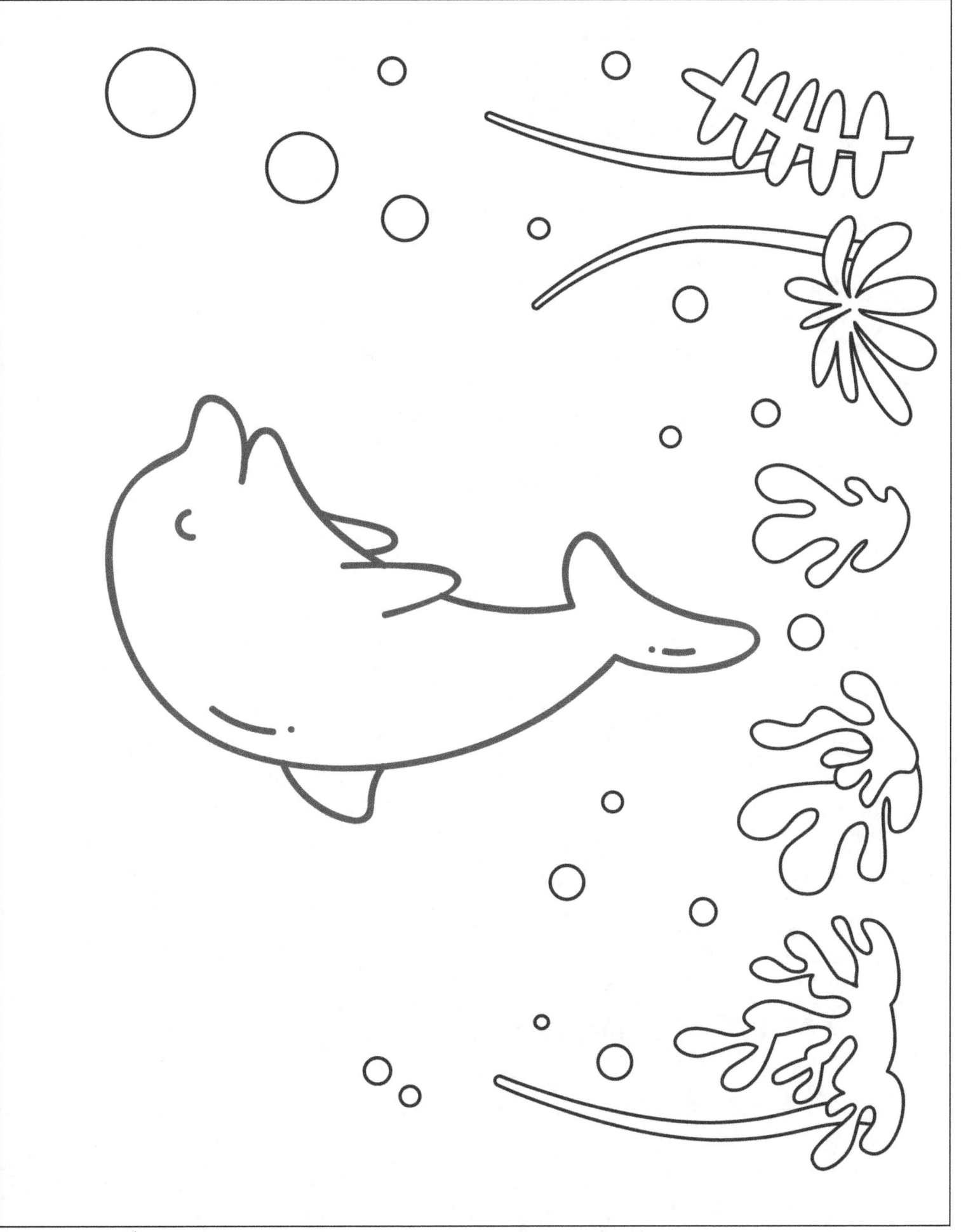

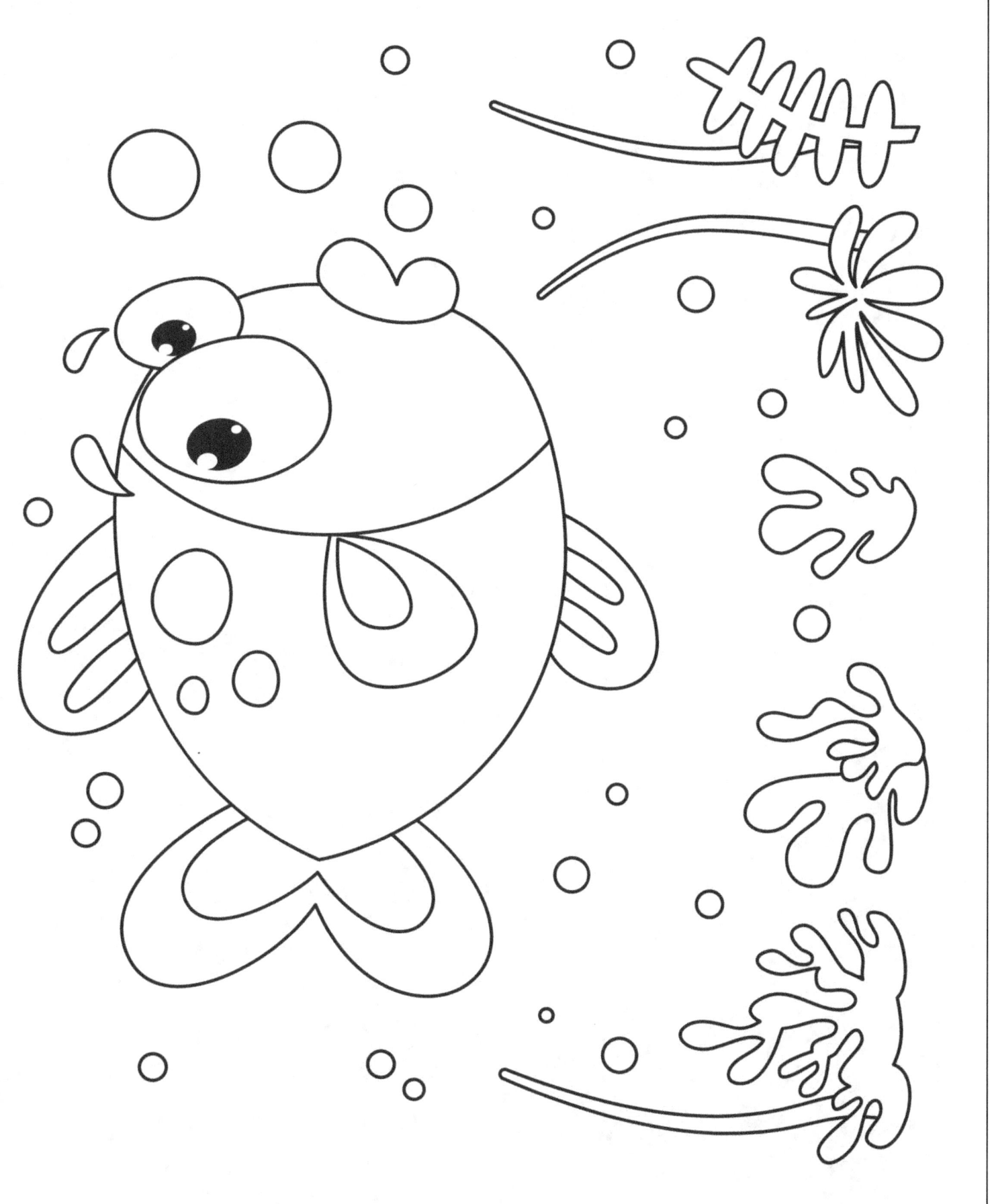

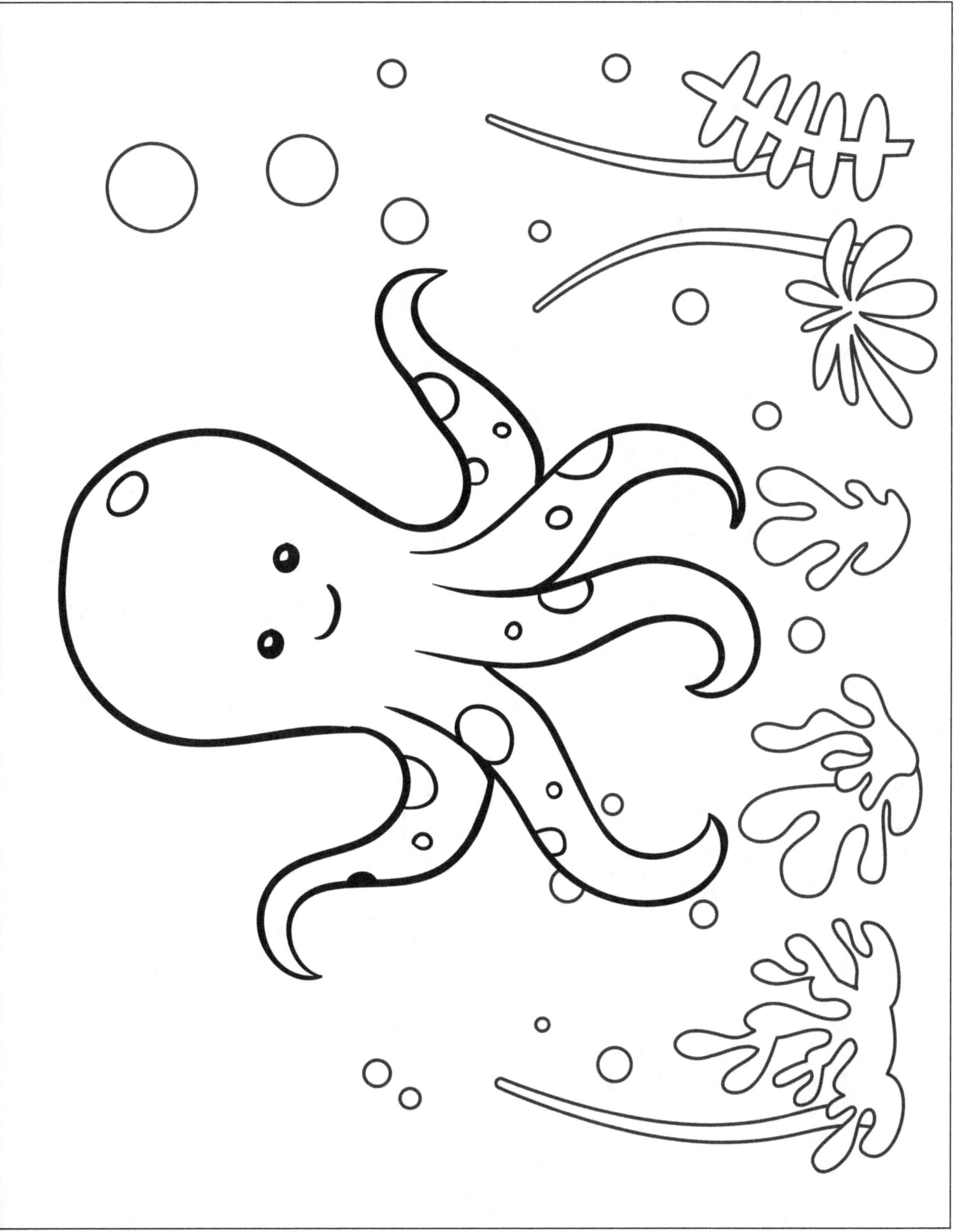

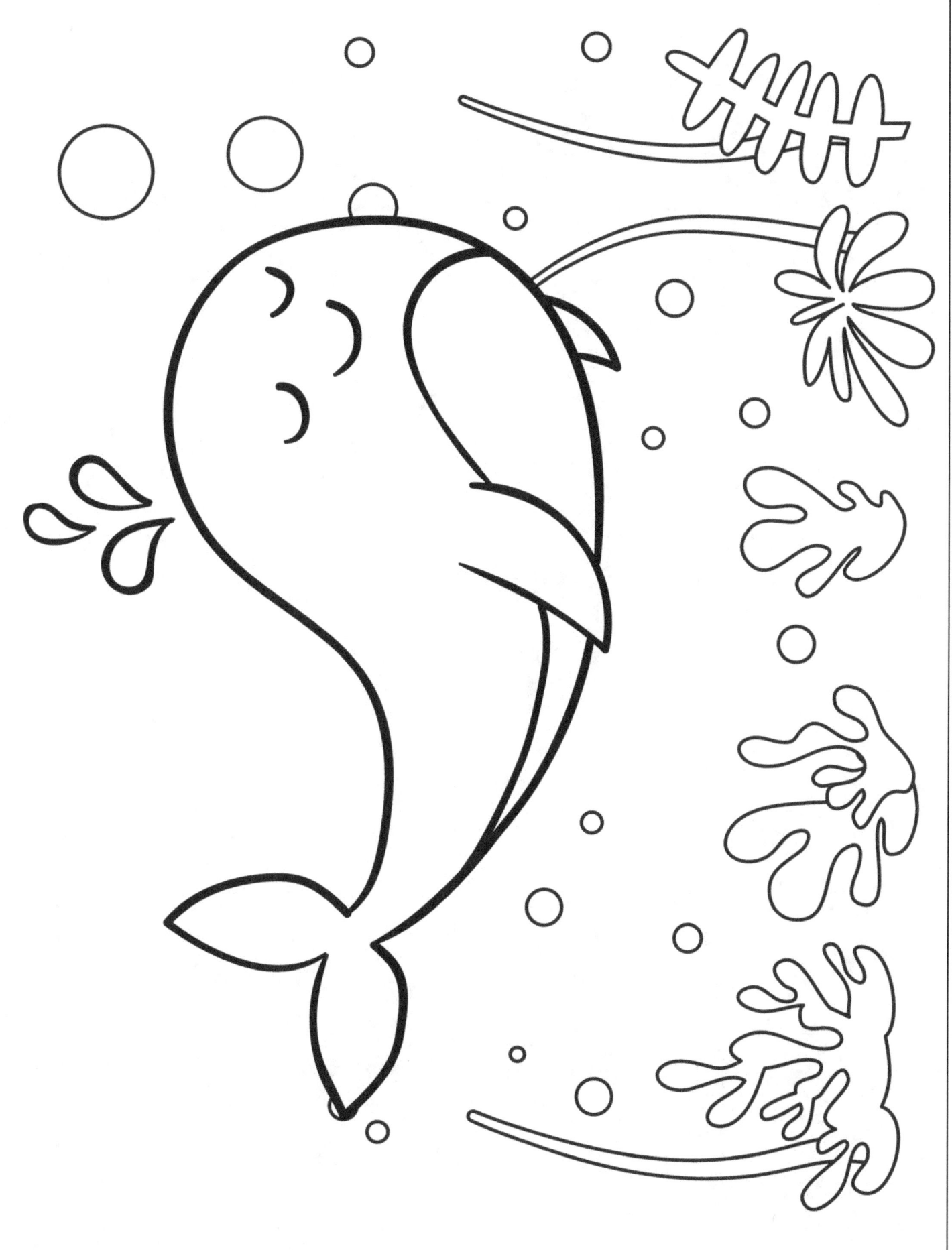

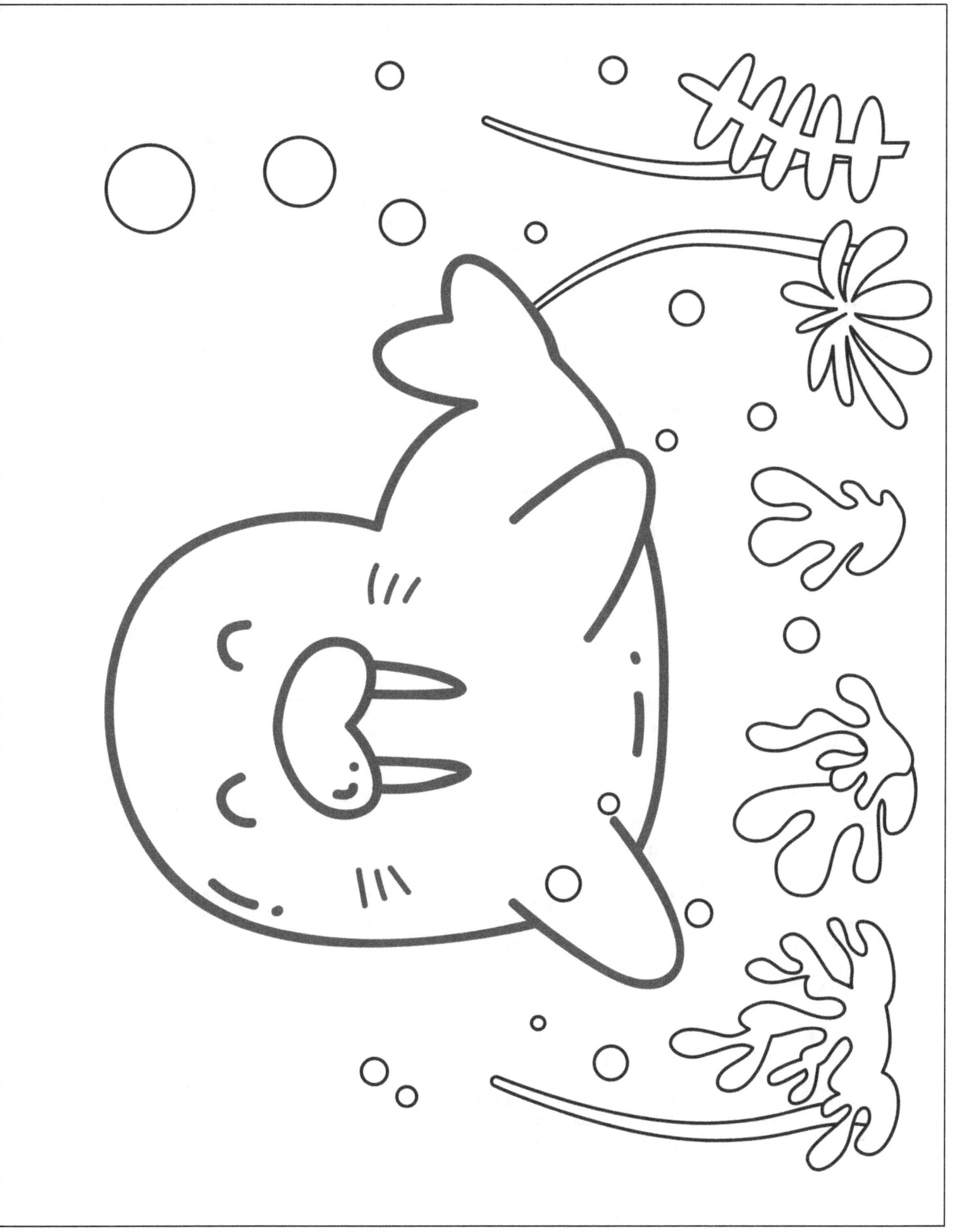

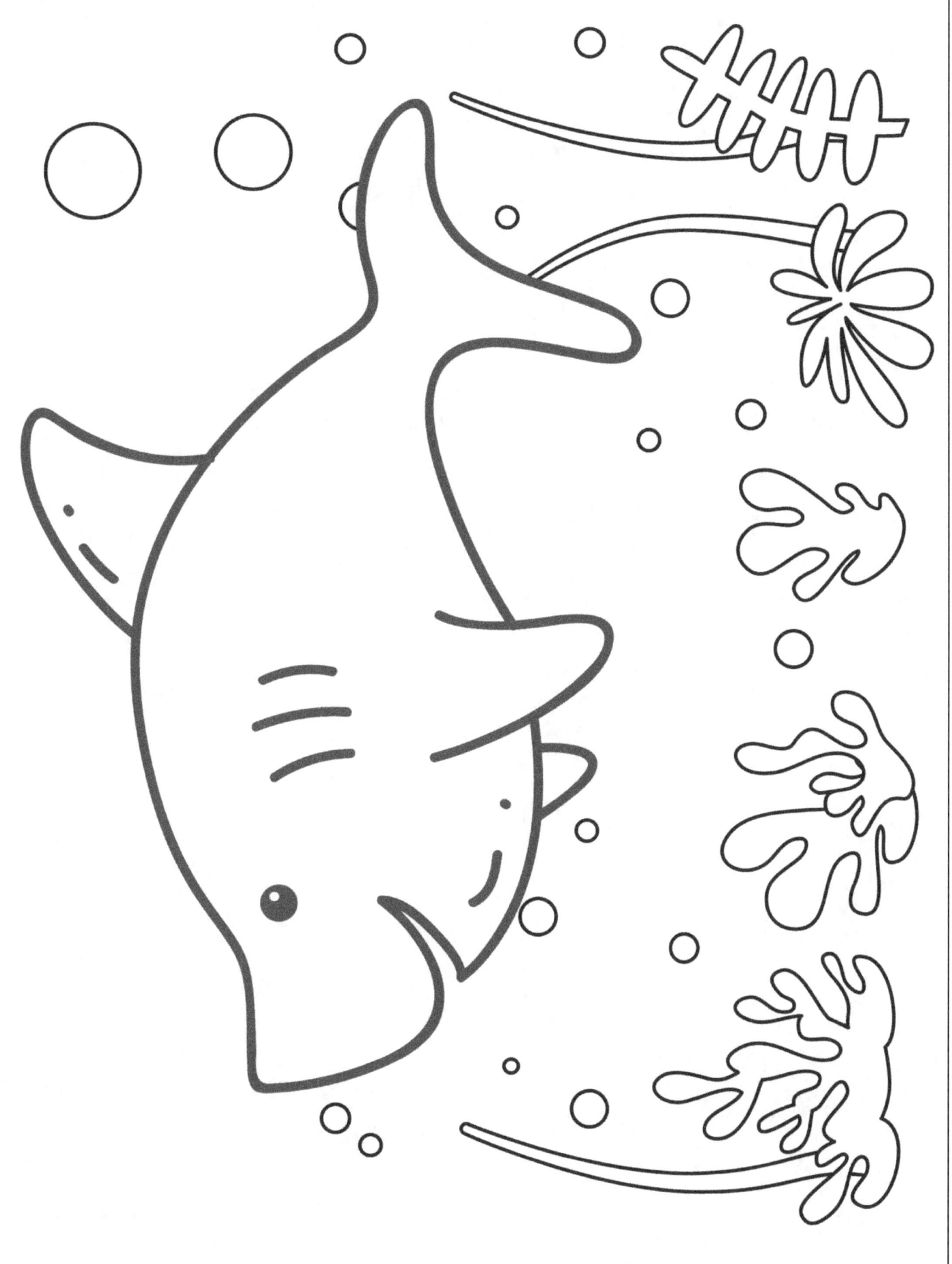

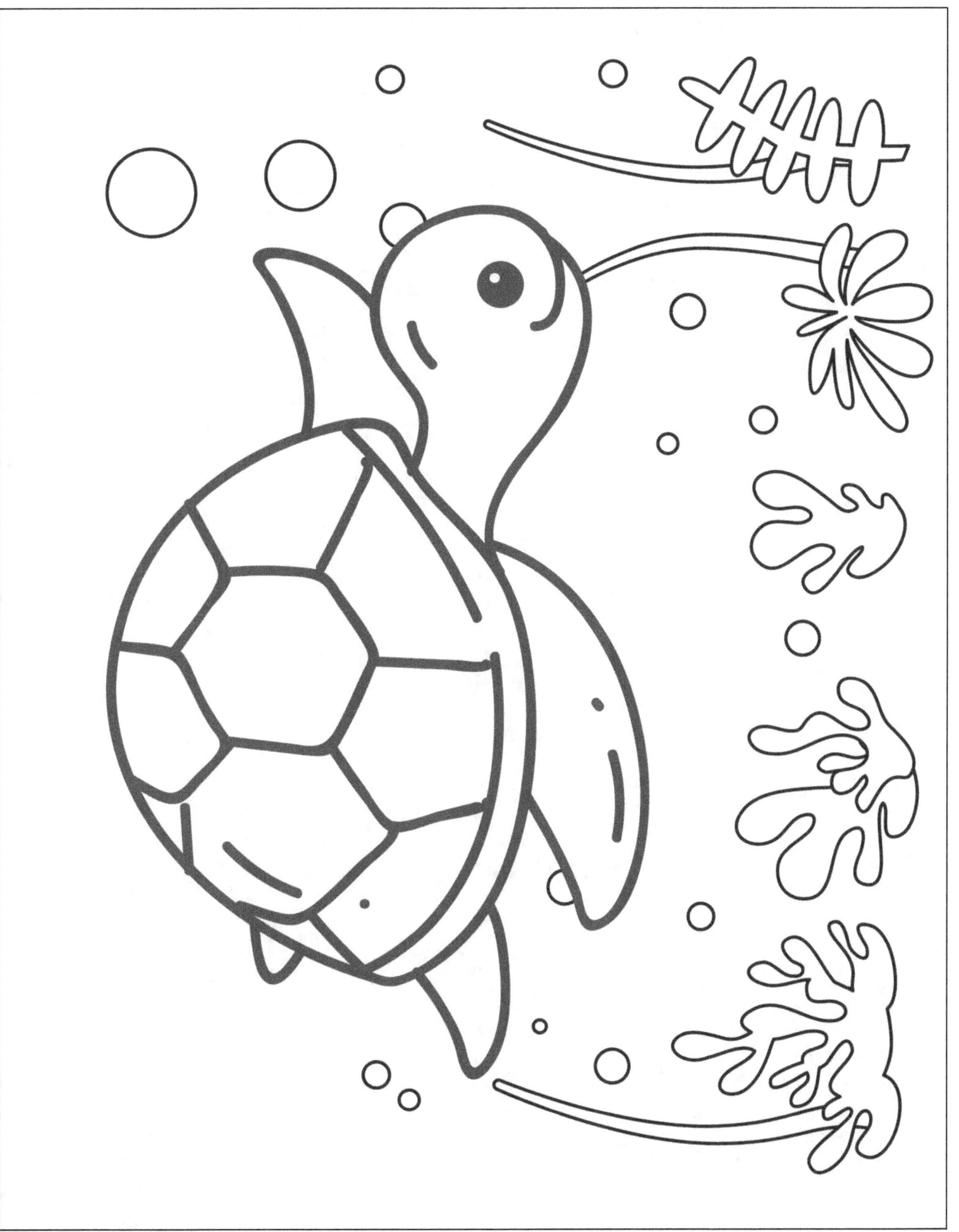

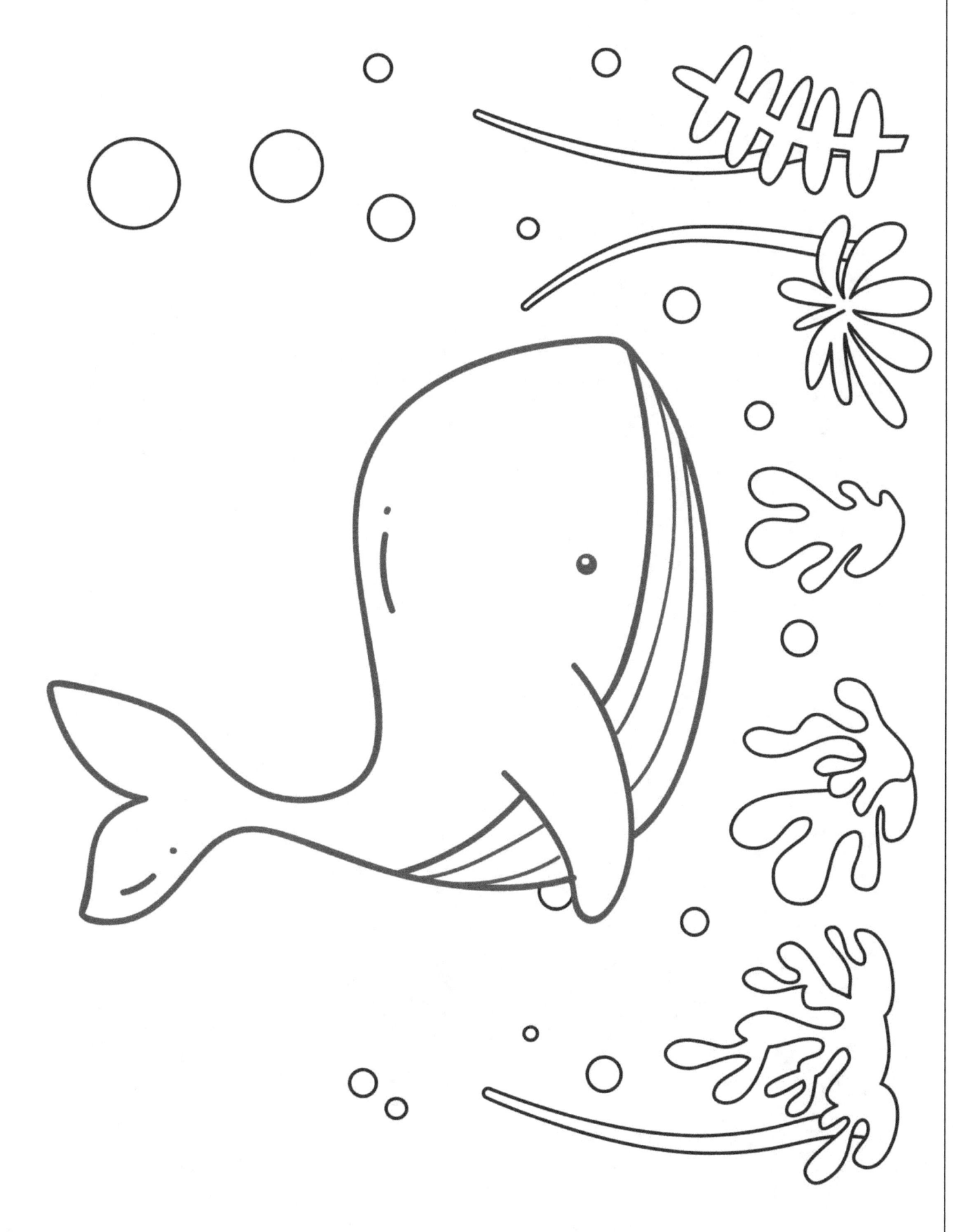

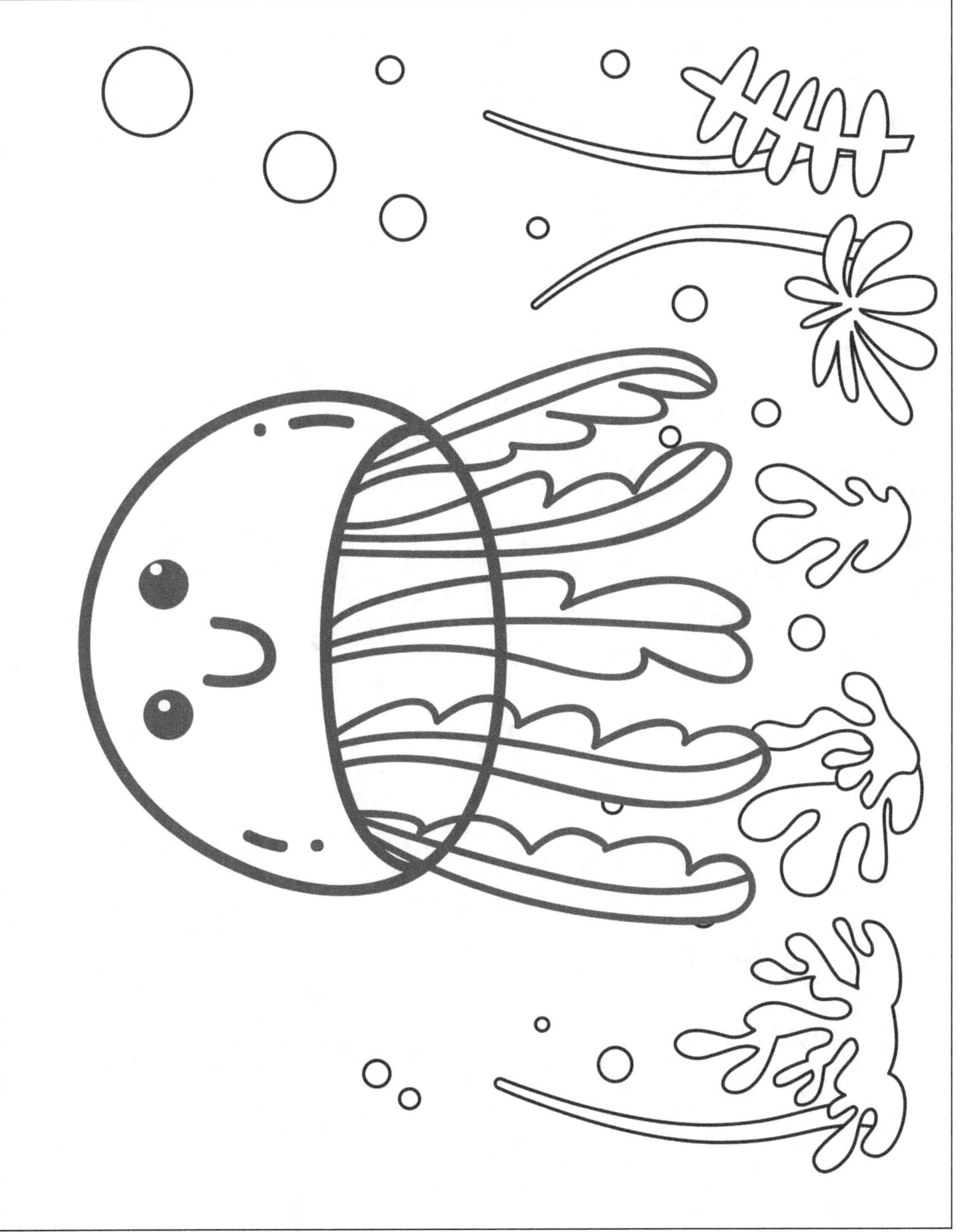

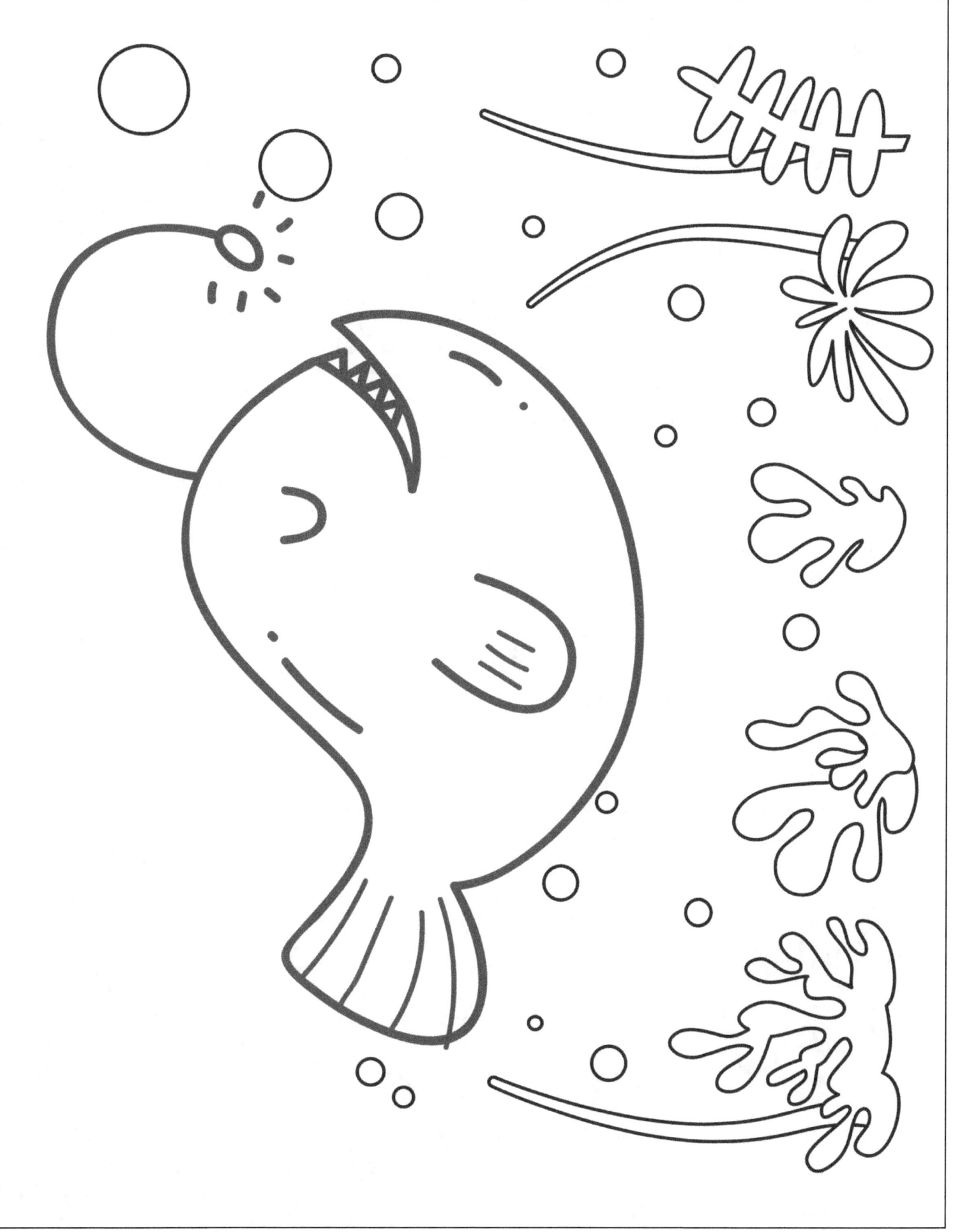

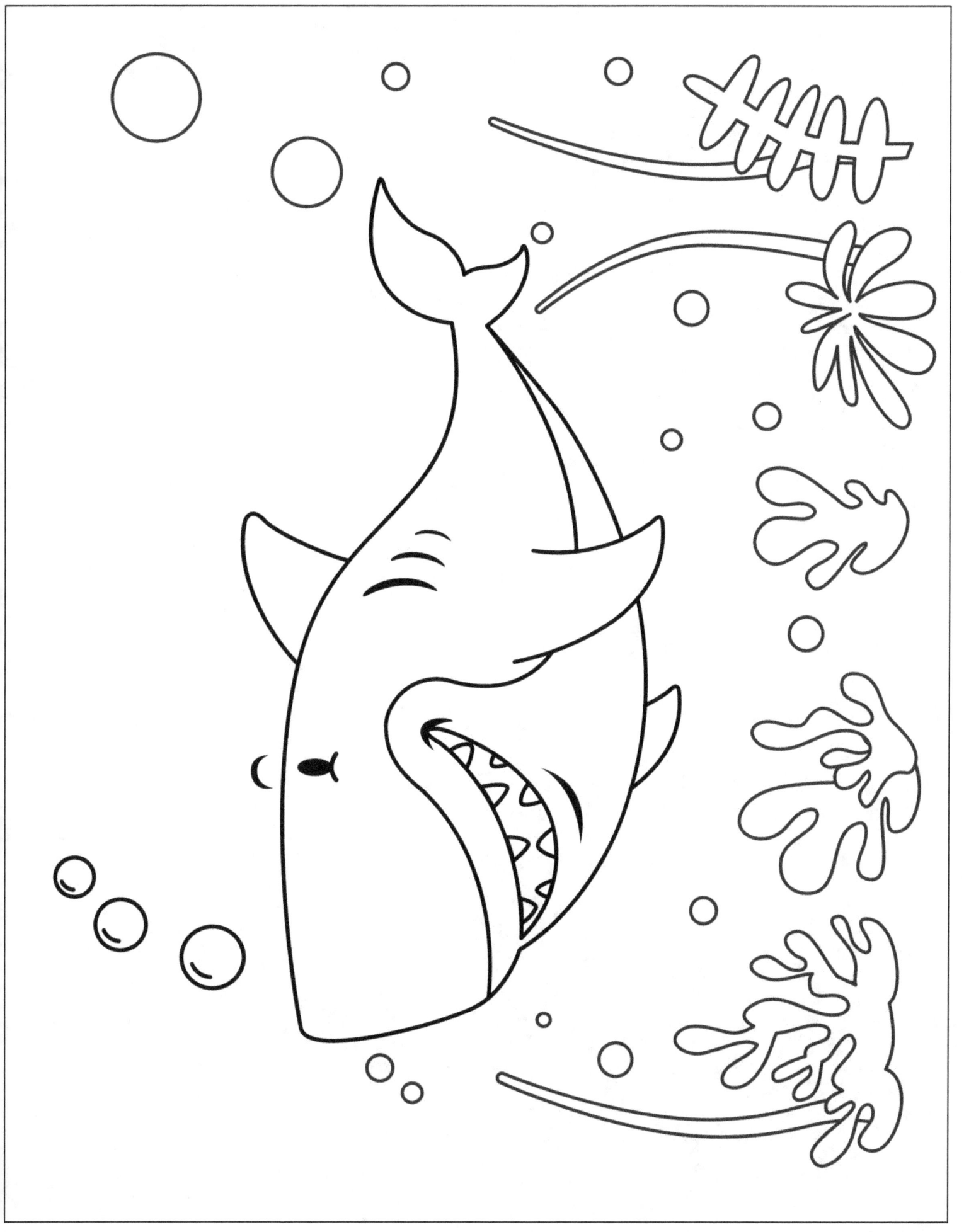

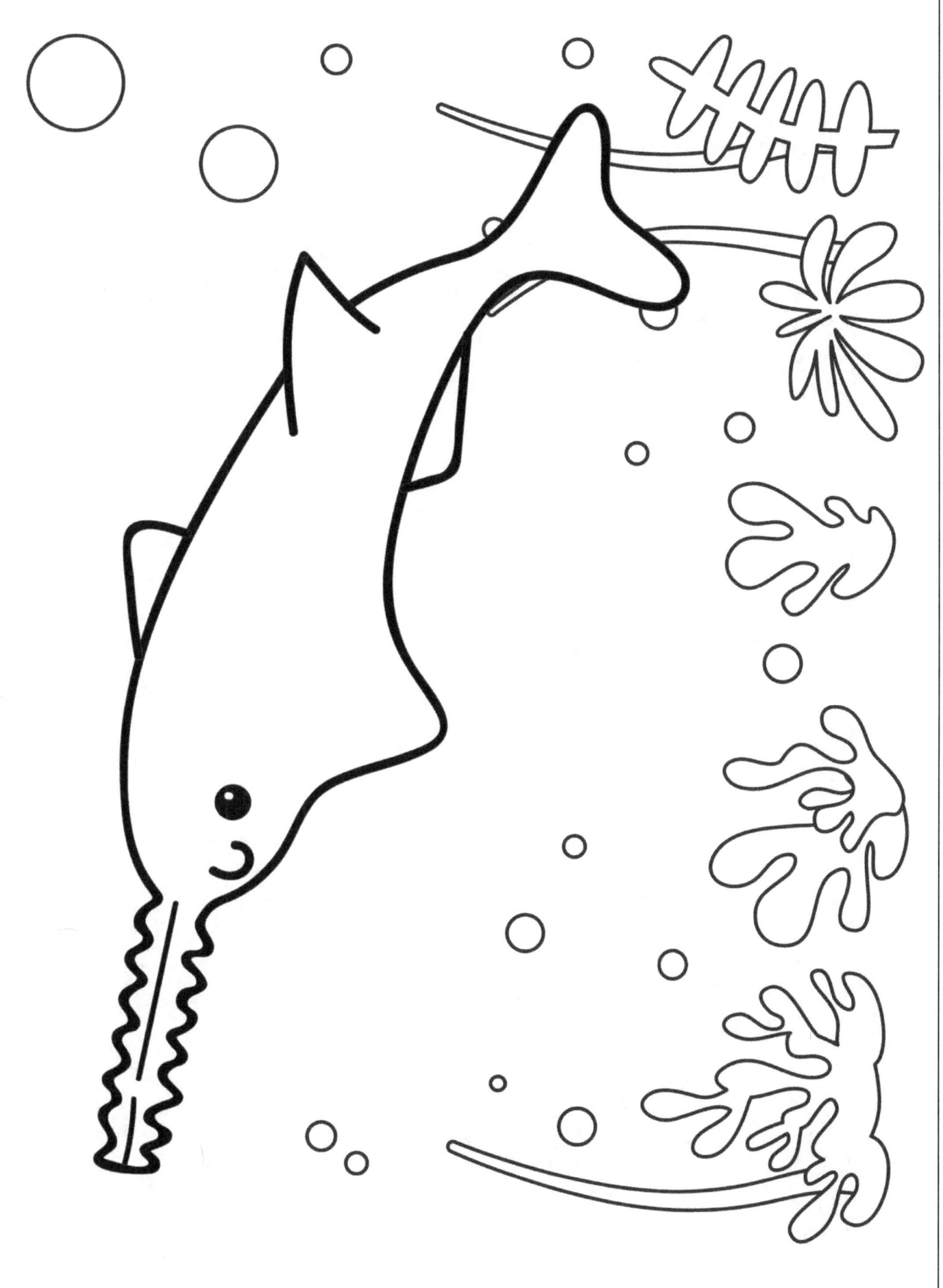

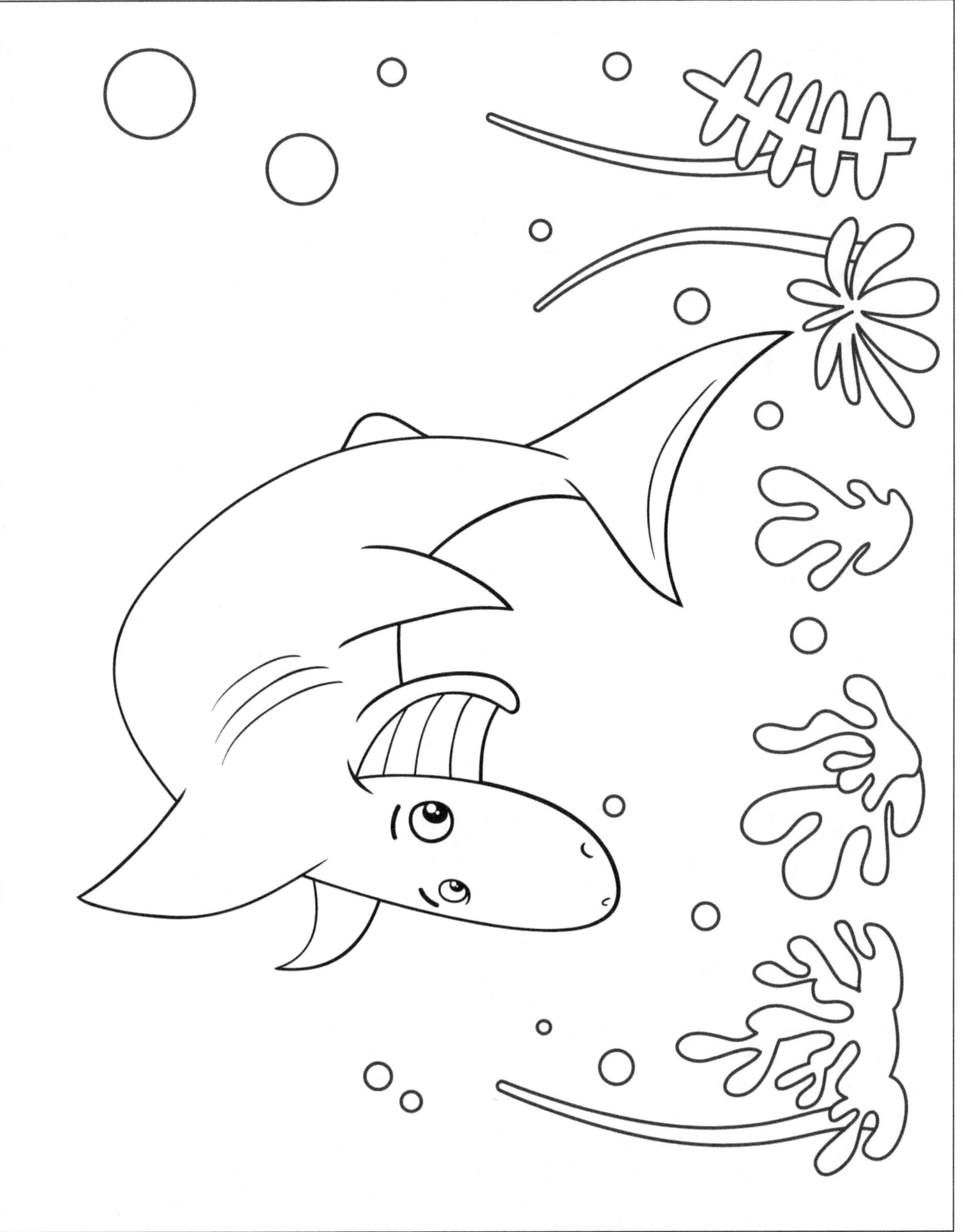

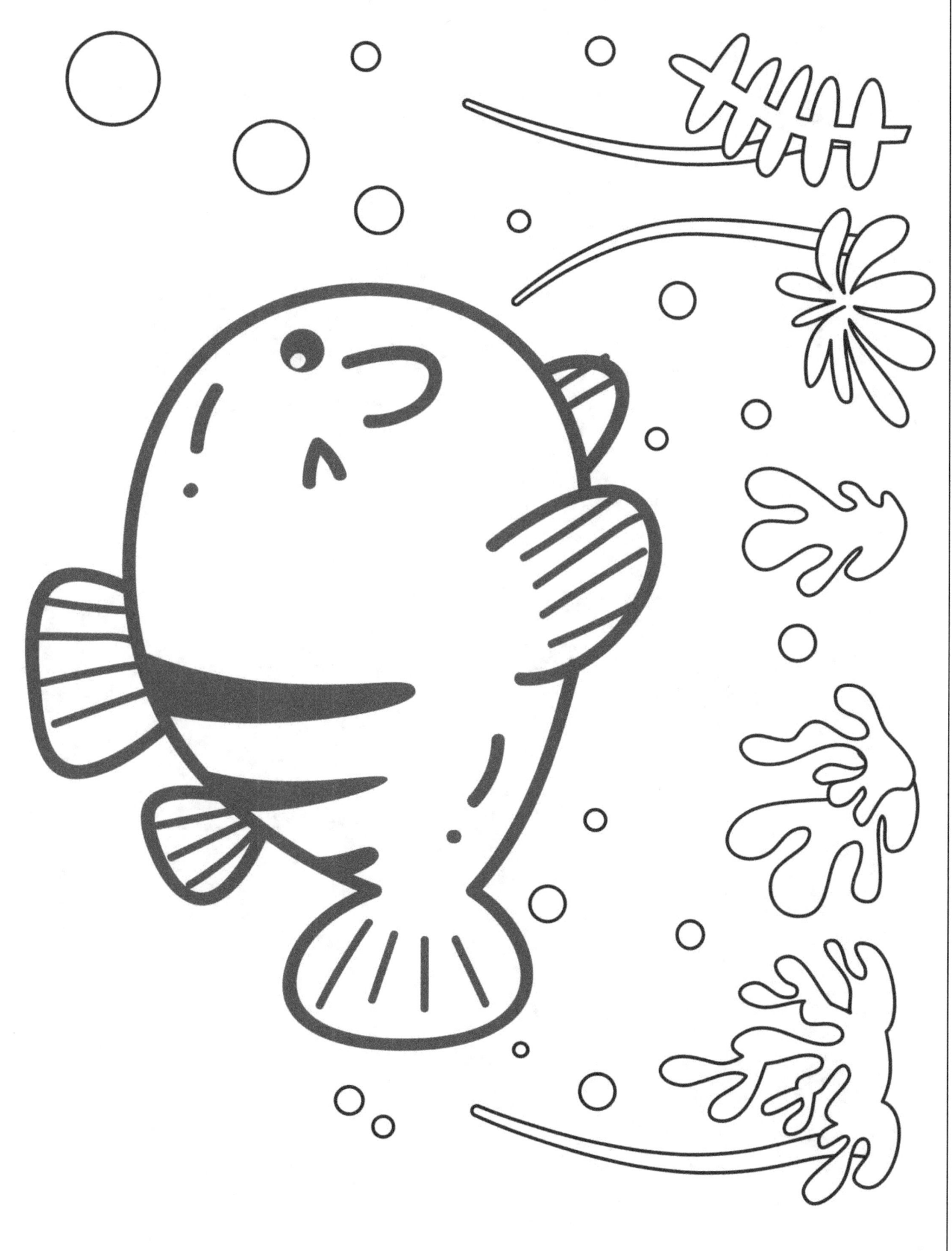

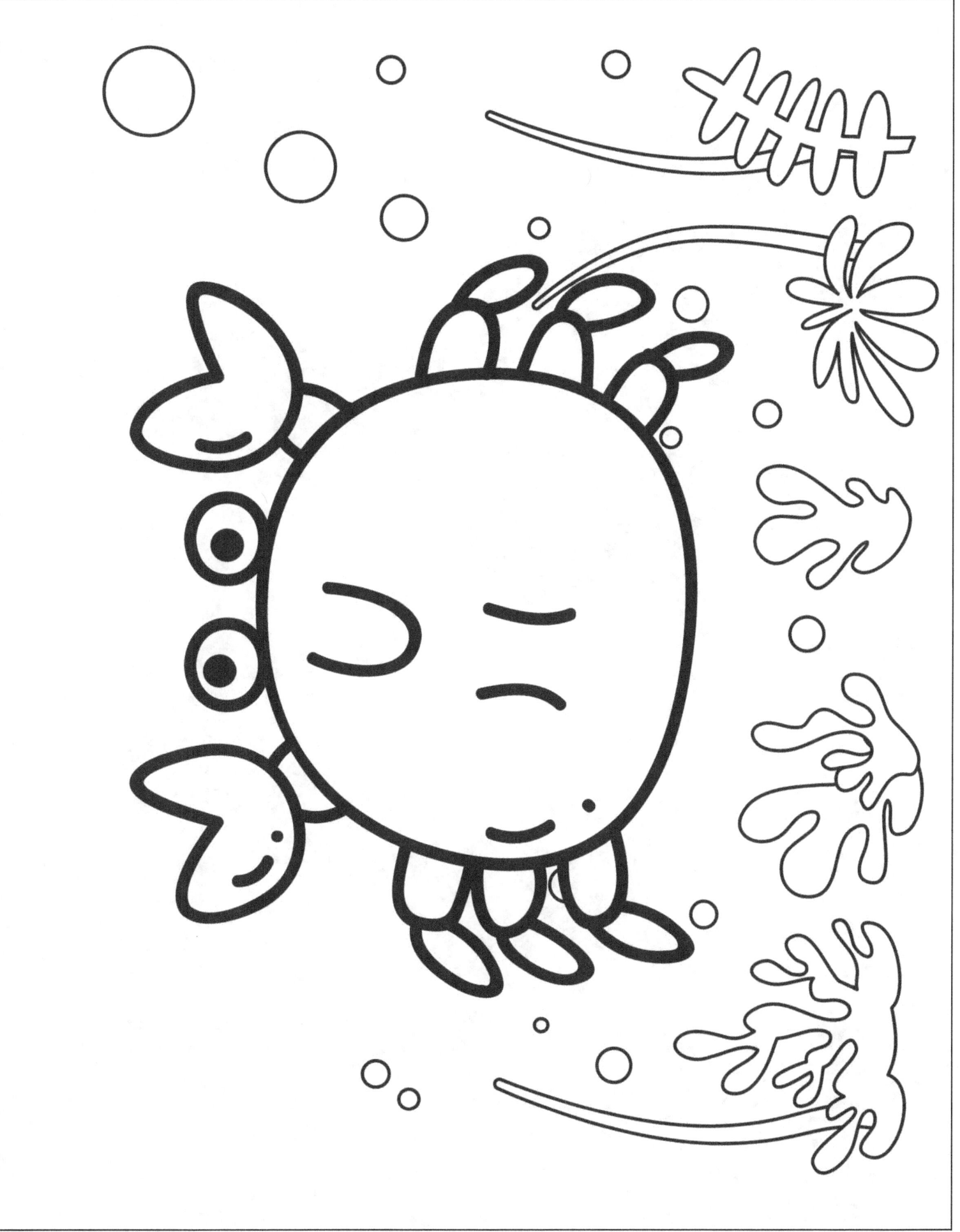

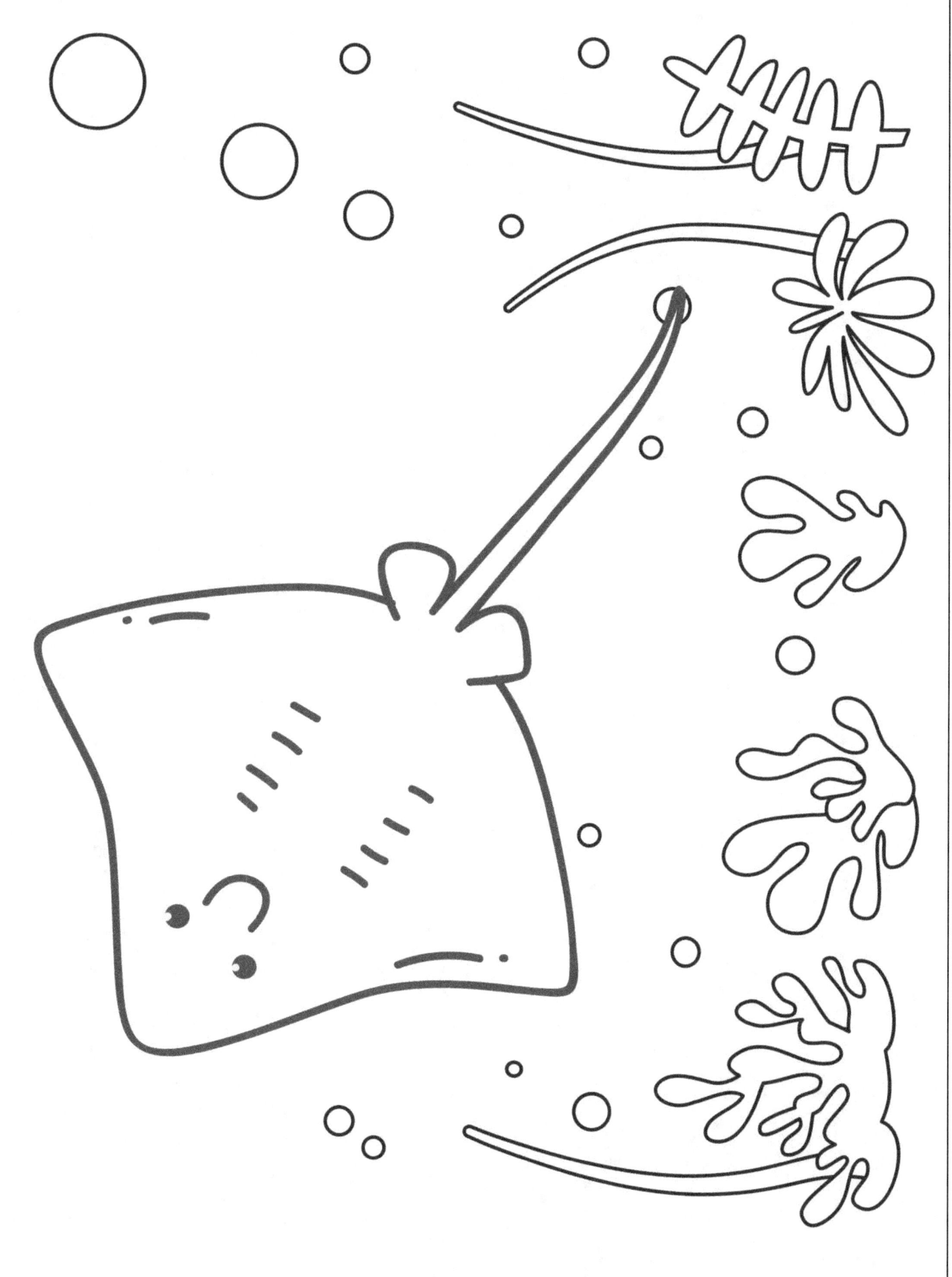

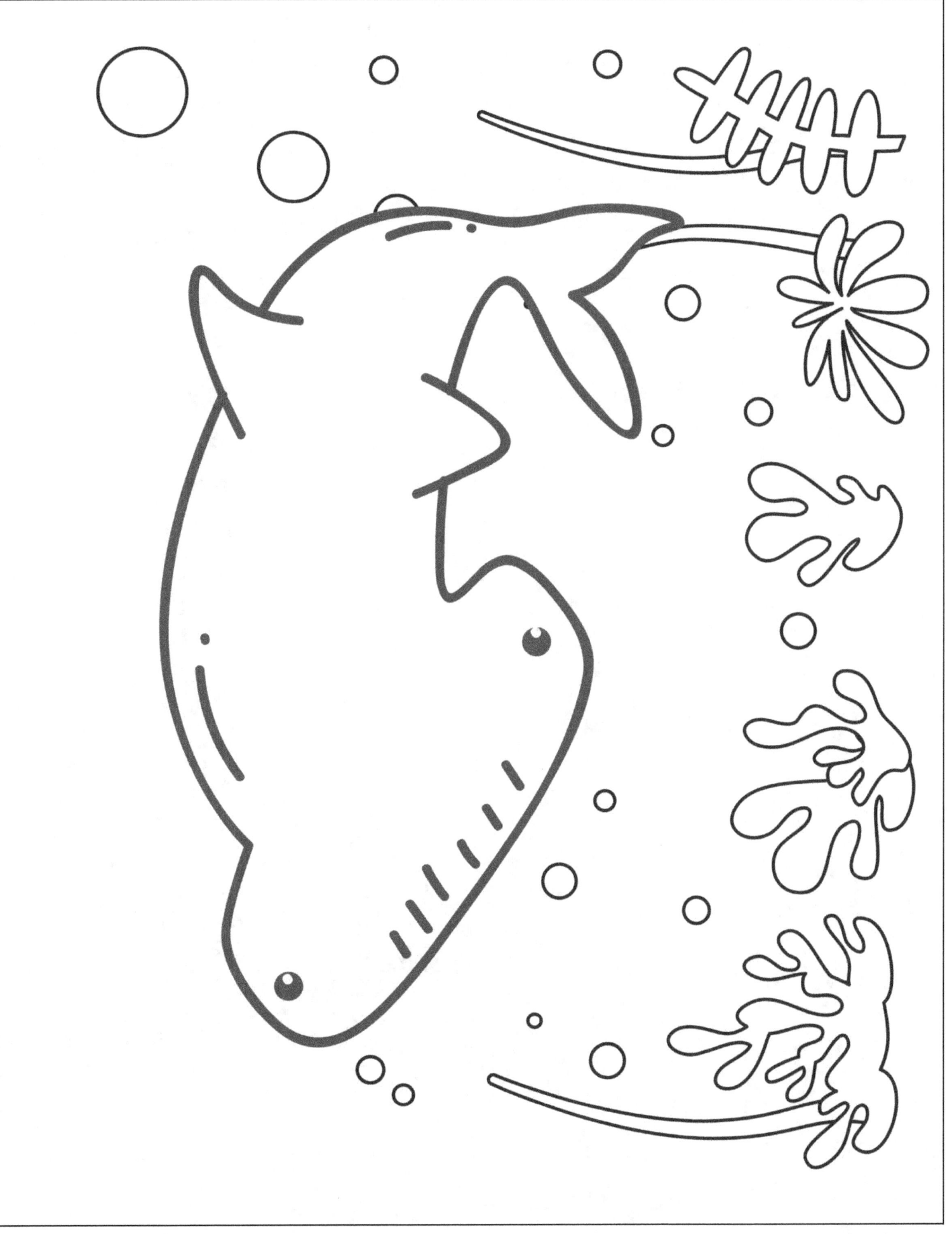

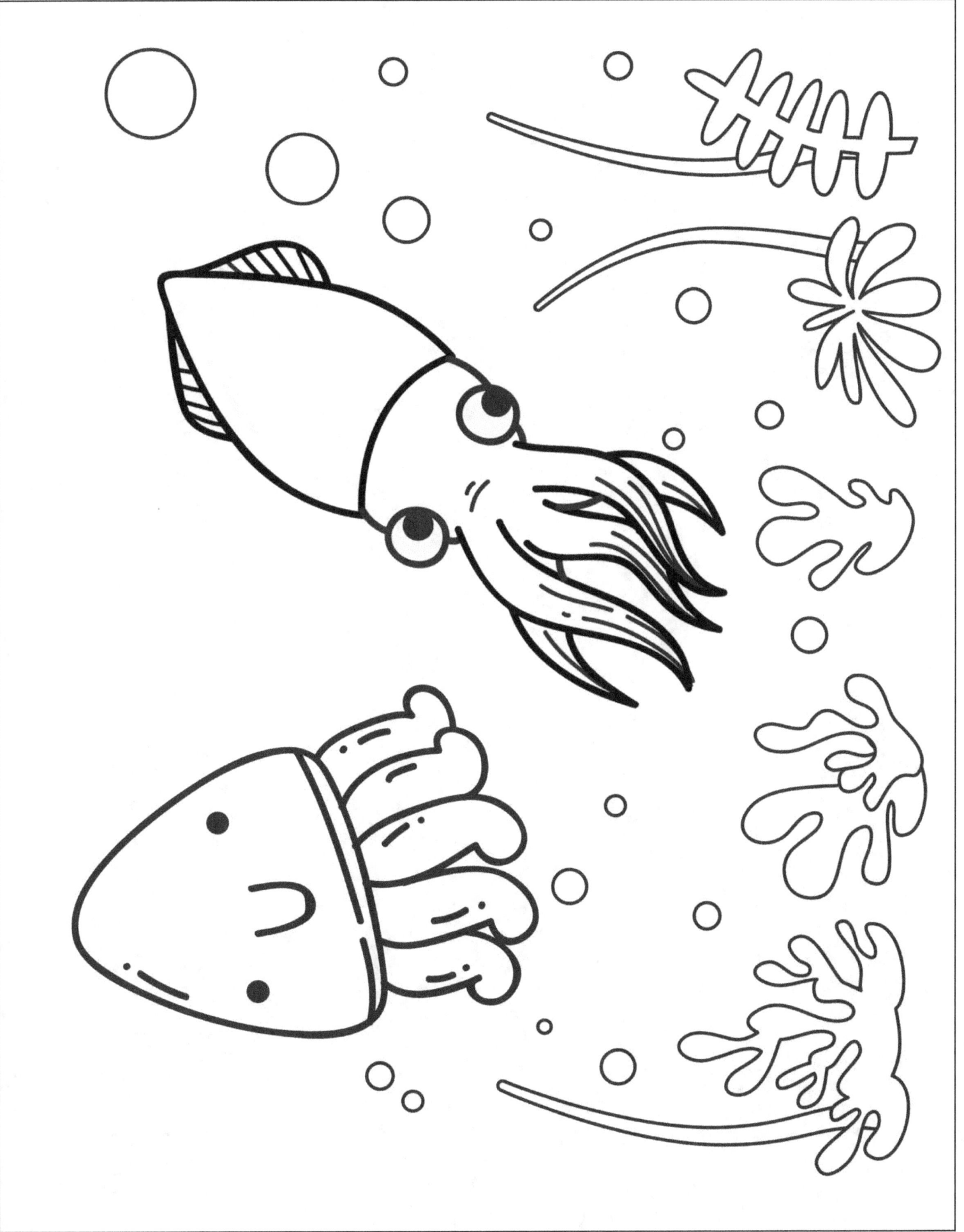

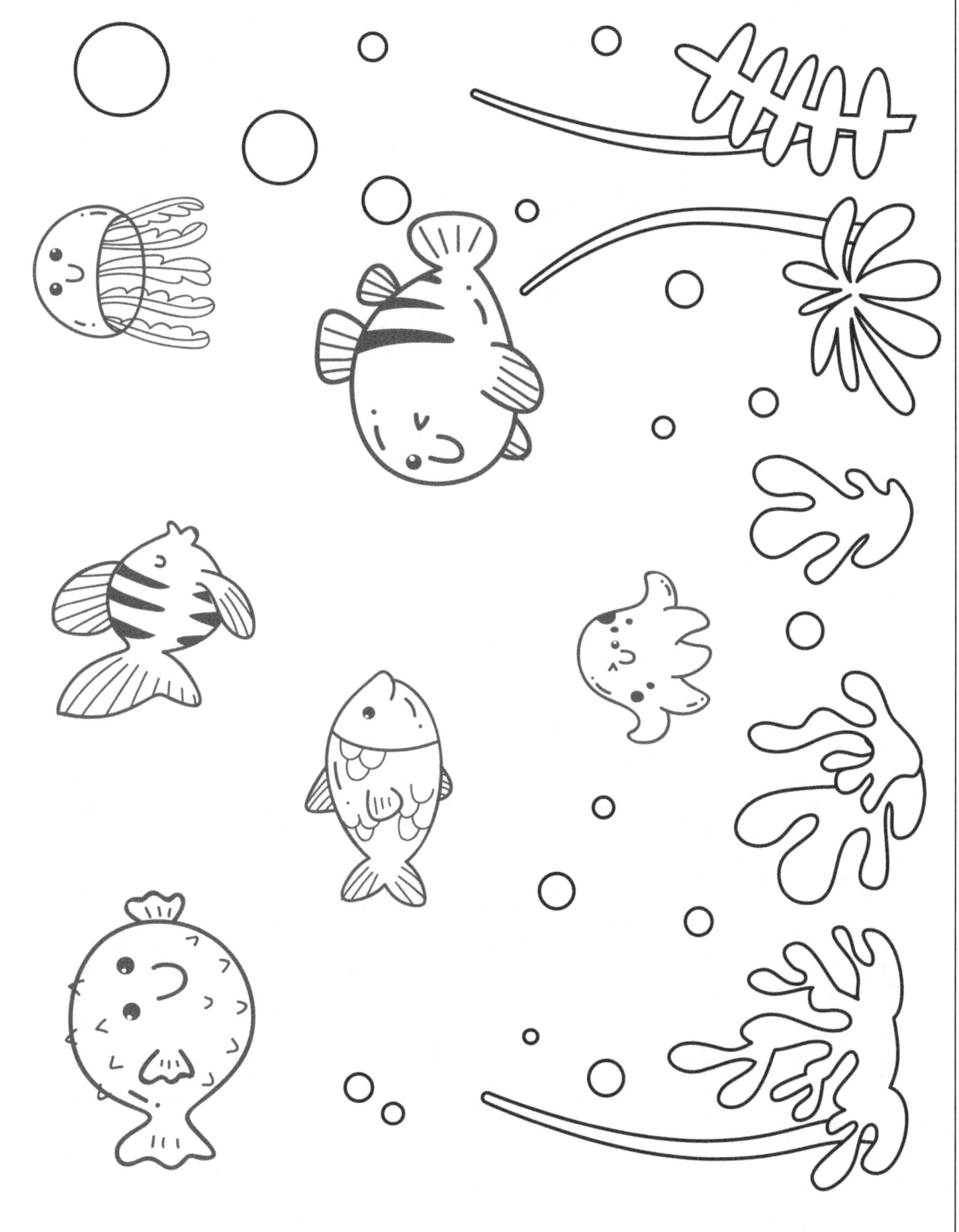

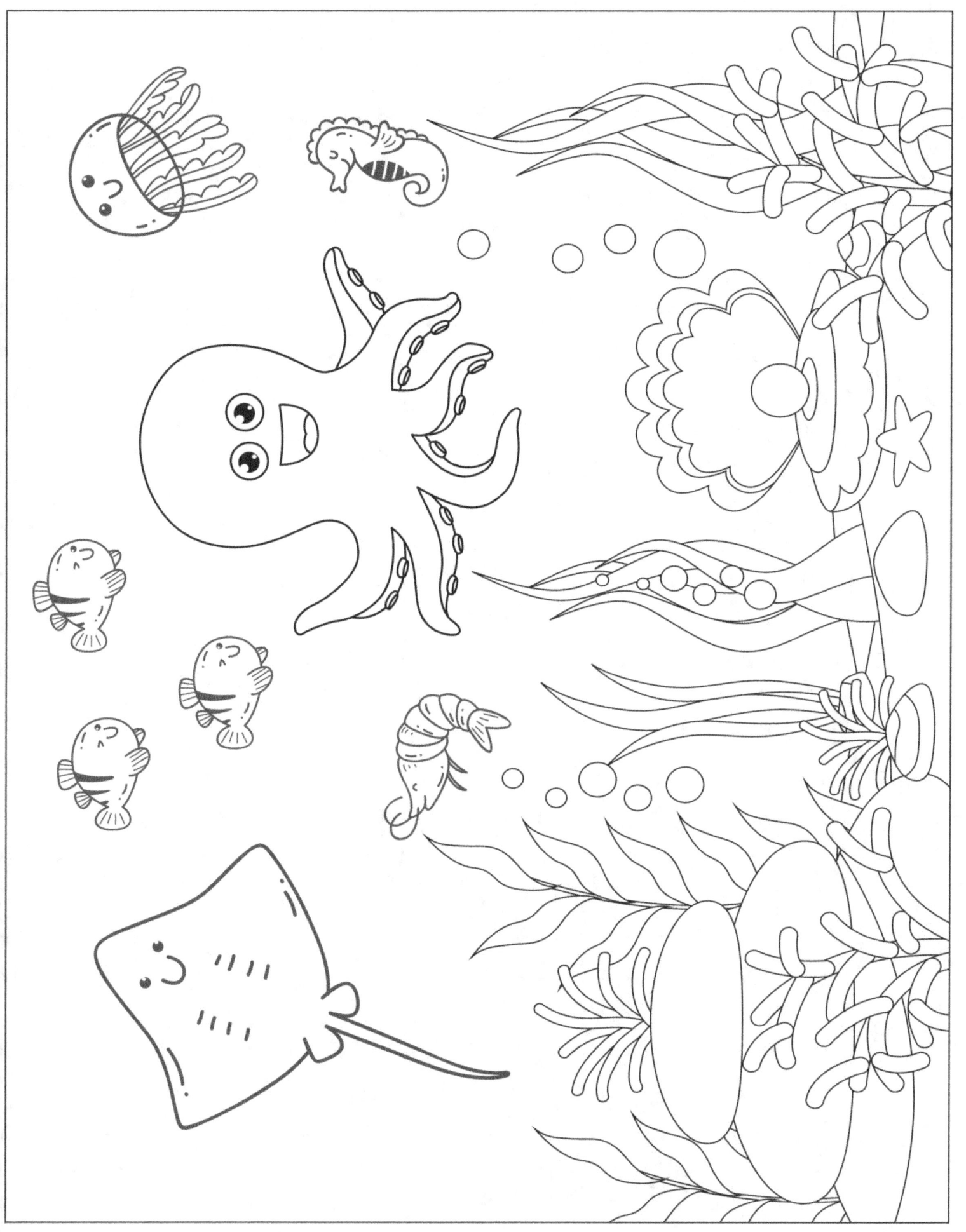

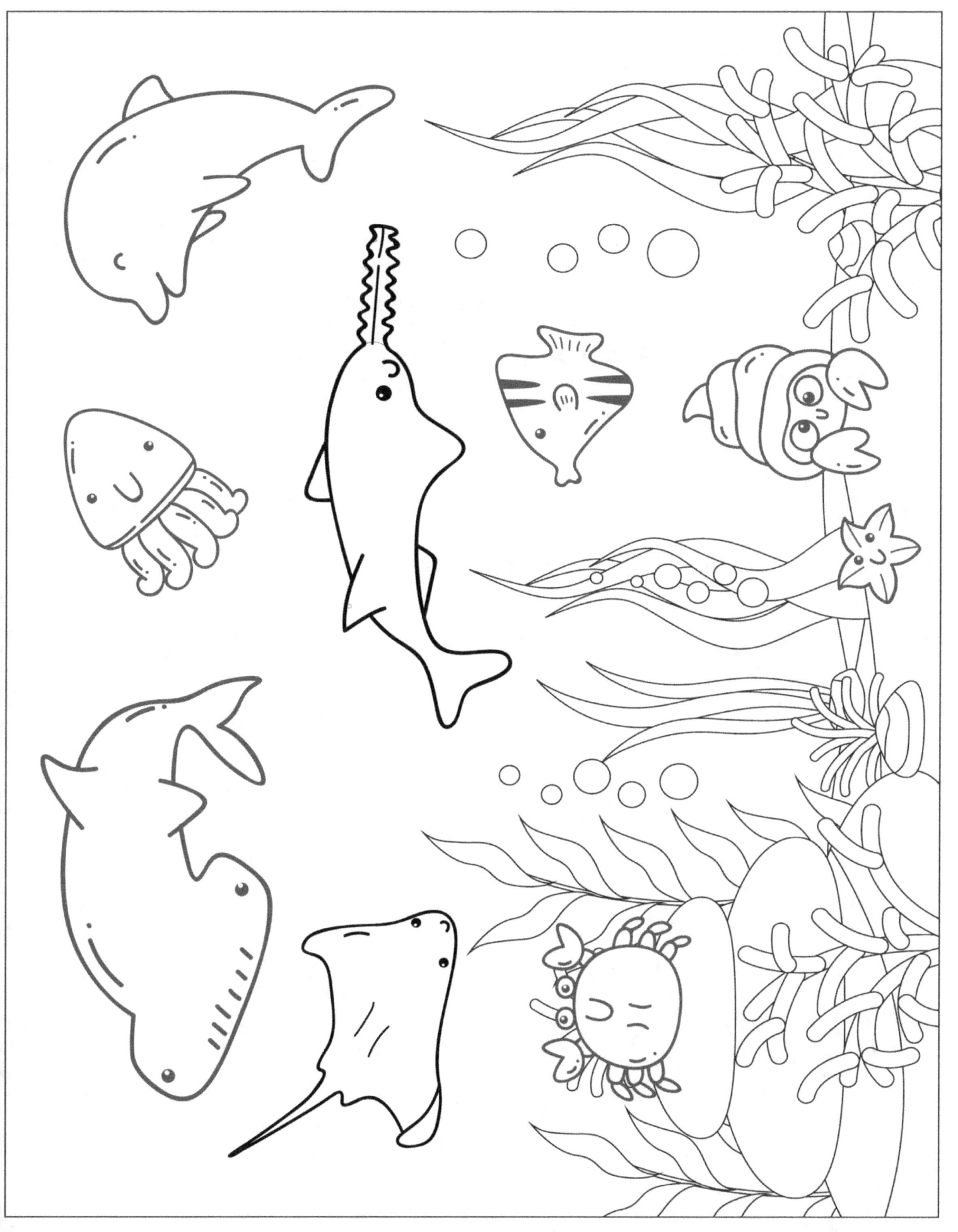

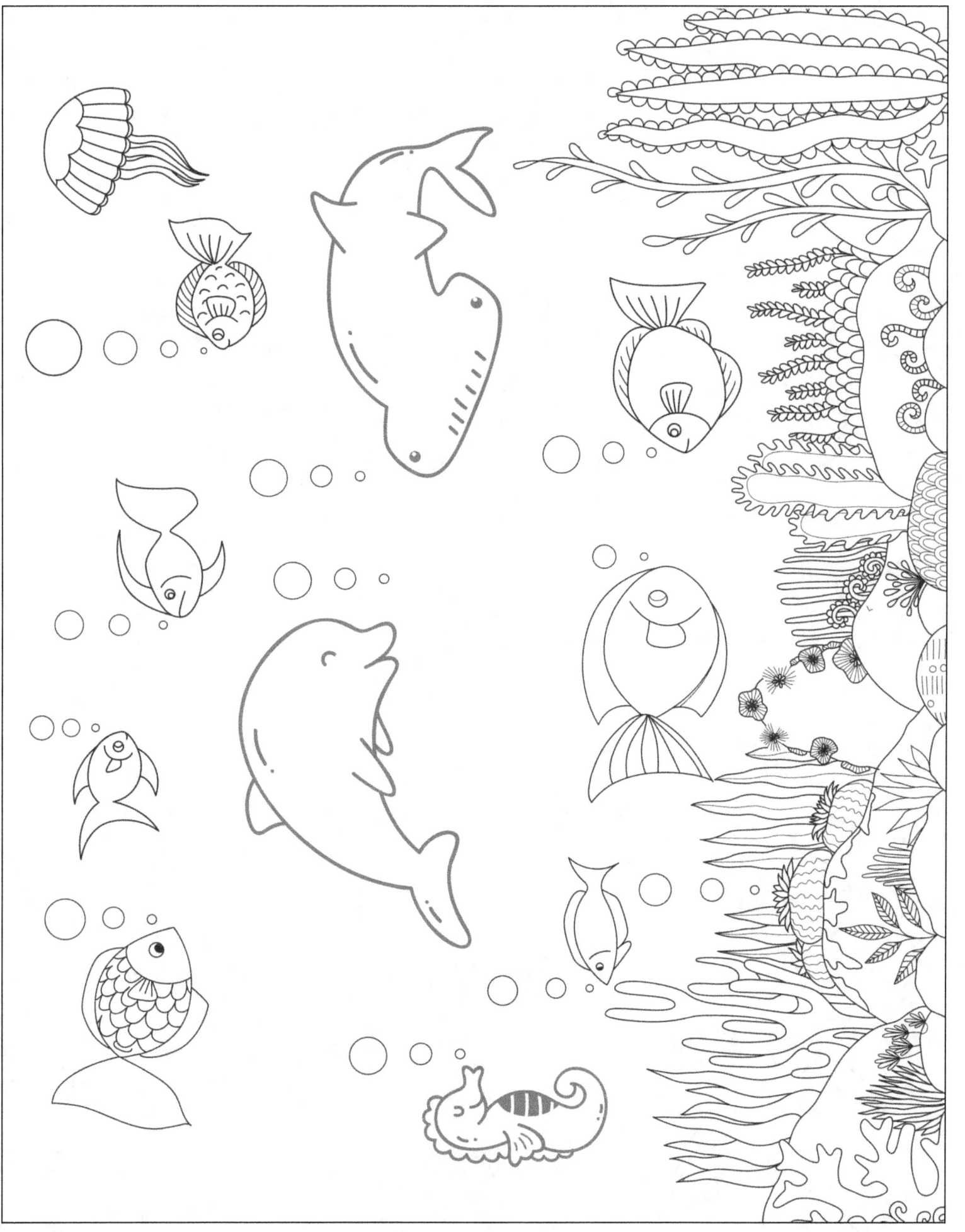

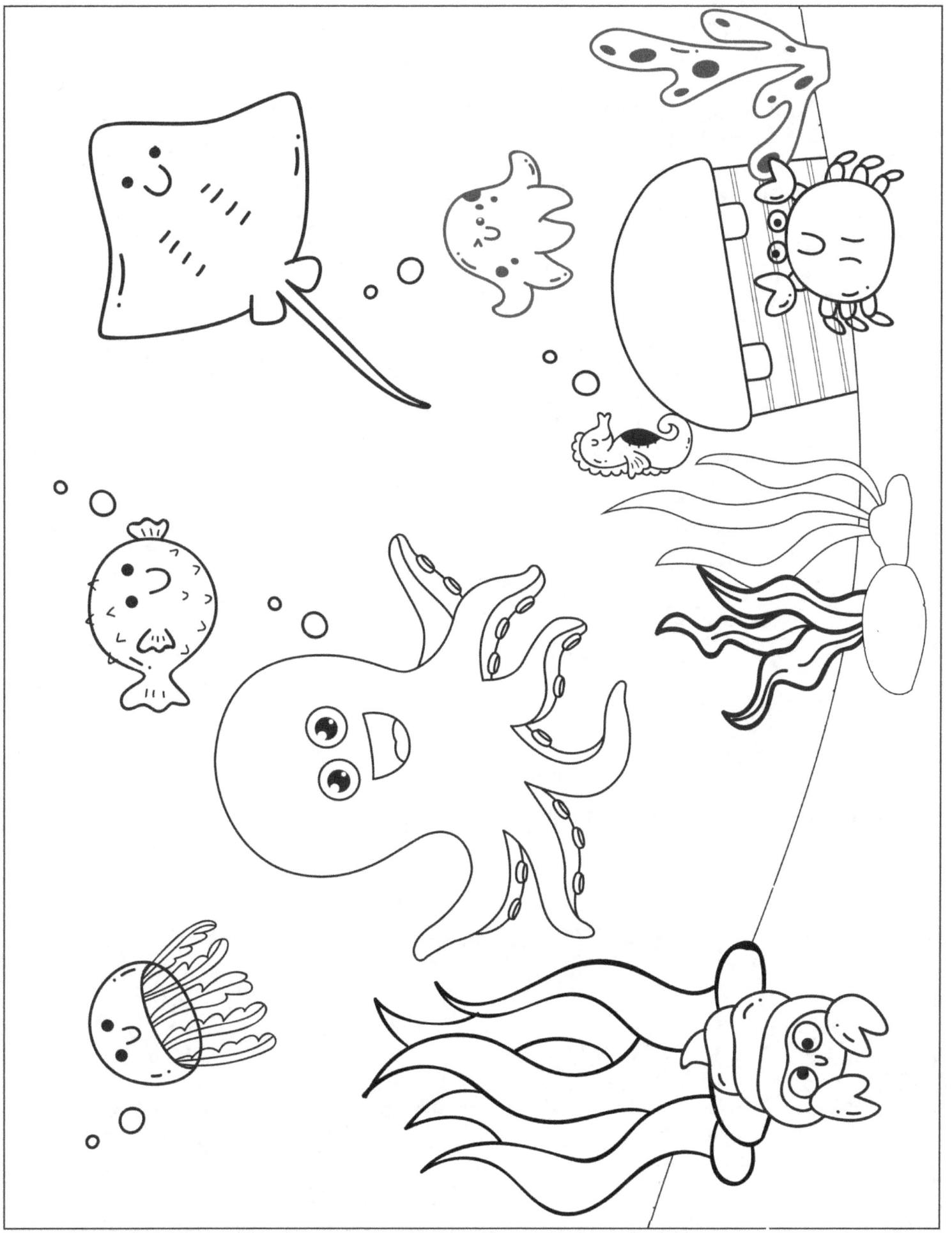

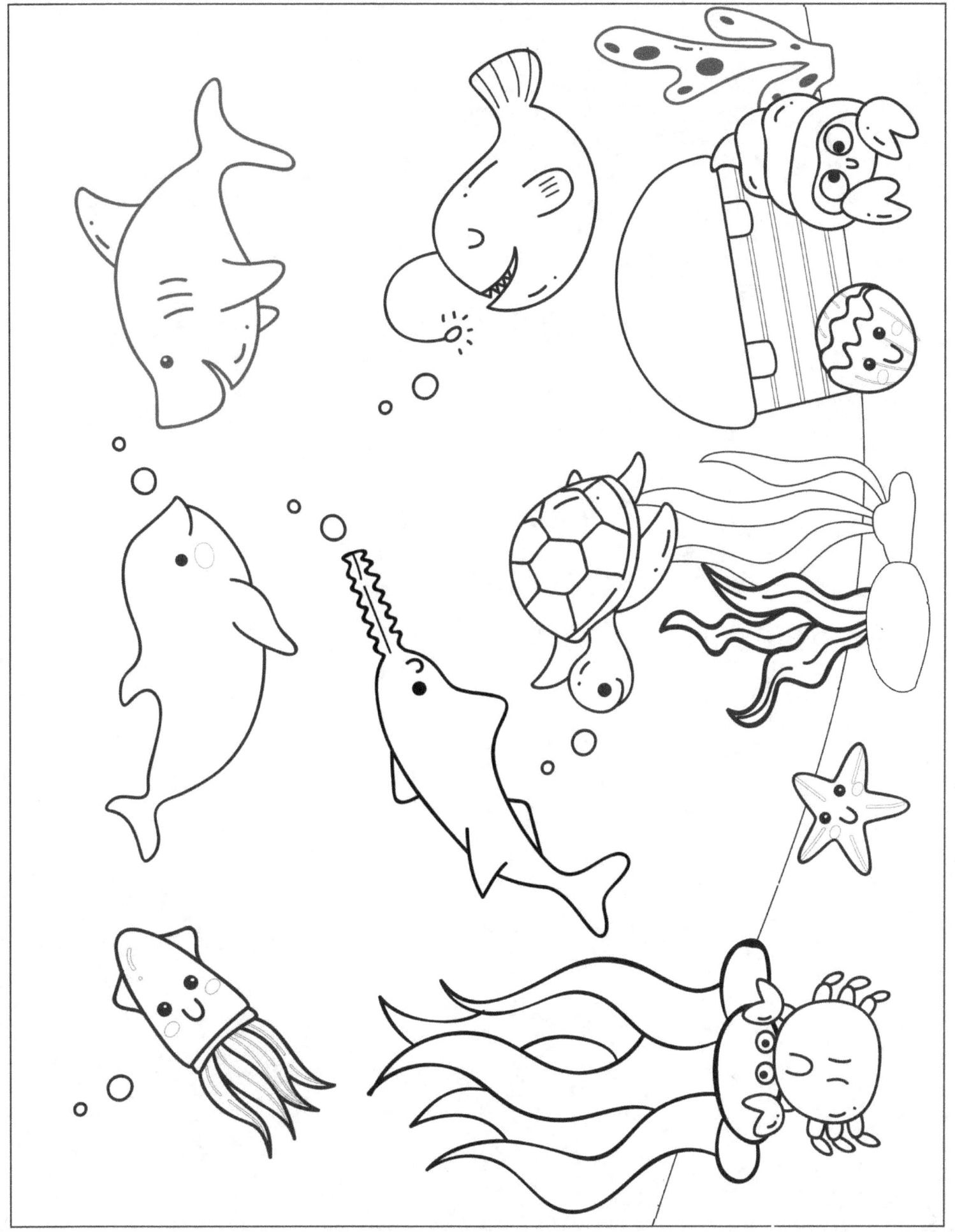

www.ingramcontent.com/pod-product-compliance
Lightning Source LLC
Chambersburg PA
CBHW080908220526
45466CB00011BA/3504